THE OTHER Shoe

JEFF MacNELLY

AVON
PUBLISHERS OF BARD, CAMELOT AND DISCUS BOOKS

THE OTHER SHOE is an original publication of Avon Books. This work has never before appeared in book form.

AVON BOOKS
A division of
The Hearst Corporation
959 Eighth Avenue
New York, New York 10019
Copyright © 1978, 1979, 1980 by Jefferson Communications, Inc.
Library of Congress Catalog Card Number:
ISBN: 0-380-75341-3

First Avon Printing, April, 1980

AVON TRADEMARK REG. U.S. PAT. OFF. AND IN OTHER COUN-
TRIES, MARCA REGISTRADA, HECHO EN U.S.A.

Printed in the U.S.A.

To Jake and Danny

Introduction

I was sitting in my red barn studio in Connecticut wondering how we could stop Jeff MacNelly. This guy was really cutting into our business. Where did he come from, anyway? A few short years ago we were all fat and happy, enjoying life and raking in the loot from drawing our cartoons. Then from nowhere this kid walks into a newspaper office in Virginia with some of the best cartoons ever drawn. I mean they were beautiful! Not only were the compositions masterfully done, but the renderings were unique, the ideas hilarious and the caricatures devastating. And to top it all off, he was tall!

That was just the beginning of Jeff MacNelly. Suddenly he was being talked about everywhere, in magazines, newspapers, massage parlors, you name it. His editorial cartoons became the envy of everyone in the business and spawned a whole school of MacNelly imitators. My own kids began studying his work and copying it.

You'd think MacNelly would be satisfied with cornering that side of the market, but no. The year before last he sneaked another one by us. A comic strip about a bird named "Shoe." It took the country by storm. In two short years it was sold to over 500 newspapers, one of the fastest growing strips in the history of the comics. Awards were heaped on him: The Pulitzer Prize (he was the youngest to ever win it), The National Cartoonists Society's Reuben, The Thomas Nast Award, to name a few.

And before the ink had even dried on his drawings, here comes a big, gorgeous edition called, THE VERY FIRST SHOE BOOK. I began putting buckshot in my bird feeder hoping to weigh down some of MacNelly's birds. It was a desperate situation. I had to do something.

My opportunity came yesterday. The phone rang and it was Jeff MacNelly. Would I write an Introduction to his next book? As I talked to him, an idea began to formulate in my mind...the way to stop MacNelly. I'd write a foreword that would send him back to the paste-up department. I'd find out how he got so tall. He probably had some pull. I'll reveal how the environmentalists feel about his excessive use of ink. I'll expose him, point out that such artistic levels don't belong in cartoons, make him an object of ridicule.

The deadline is next week. I'd better get to work on it.

Mort Walker

Foreword

This volume is the second collection of Jeff MacNelly's SHOE. It represents the Best of SHOE from the winter of 1978 through the winter of 1979. During this period it became the most popular new comic strip in a decade, appearing in newspapers across the United States and around the world. At this same time, Jeff was awarded both the Pulitzer Prize and the "Reuben," the Oscar of the international cartoon world. Clearly, the following pages show a great cartoonist working at the peak of his skills.

We are grateful to another great cartoonist—Mort Walker—for his lambent Introduction. As the creator of Beetle Bailey, Hi and Lois, Boner's Ark and Sam and Silo, Mort Walker is probably the best-known cartoonist in the world today. He is indisputably the most tireless supporter of his profession, pouring time and money into projects that will promote comic art and public appreciation of those who create it. If he were not in the prime of his creative life, he would doubtless be known as the grand old man of the comics.

Our thanks also to Nancy Neiman and Judith Riven of Avon, whose firm hands on the editorial tiller guided this book smoothly to publication; to Bob Reed, Don Michel and Walter Mahoney of the Chicago Tribune-New York News Syndicate, without whose indefatigible salesmanship SHOE would have been less of an international triumph; to Rita MacNelly, whose radiant enthusiasm has been a critical ingredient throughout; and to my partner Jane Freeman, without whom nothing gets done around here.

August 1979
Vienna, Virginia

Neal B. Freeman
Jefferson Communications, Inc.

Car Care Q and A
by the Perfesser

Q. What can I do about the loud noise in my transmission?

A. Simple. I've found that the noise will go away instantly...

when you turn up your radio.

WAIT...BEFORE WE GO I HAVE TO TAKE OUT THE GARBAGE...

HOW CAN YOU TELL WHICH PILE IS THE GARBAGE?

EASY.

THE GARBAGE IS THE NEAT PILE.

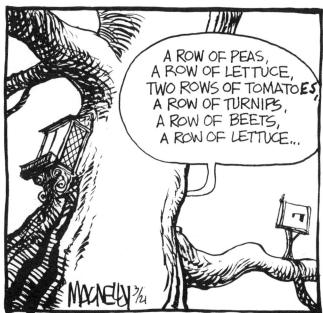

4

YOU SURE GOT A LOT OF SEEDS HERE, PERFESSER...

YUP.

IT'S MOSTLY THAT HEALTH FOOD STUFF, THOUGH.

WELL, THAT'S THE BASIC IDEA, SHOE...

3/28

BUT, IF YOU LIKE, I'LL PUT IN A ROW OF FRENCH FRIES FOR YOU.

WELL, I DON'T KNOW ABOUT YOU, BUT I AIN'T EATIN' THIS YUKKY STUFF...

LOOK WHAT WE GOT HERE... BROCCOLI! RHUBARB —YECK!... BRUSSELS SPROUTS... BEETS!... NOTHIN' GOOD TO EAT.

3/29

DON'T ANY OF THESE CLOWNS PLANT PIZZA?

7

9

I GOTTA HIRE A SECRETARY...

WHAT FOR?

WELL, FOR ONE THING SHE'D ANSWER THIS PHONE....I'M A BIG-DEAL EXECUTIVE, AND I CAN'T BE BOTHERED ANSWERING MY OWN PHO...

RING!

I'LL GET IT, MR. BIG DEAL.

HELLO, SHOE'S OFFICE...

SORRY, HE'S BUSY. YOU WANT TO TALK TO HIS SECRETARY?... WELL, OKAY, BUT YOU'LL HAVE TO HOLD ON FOR A DAY OR TWO.

TAKE THIS DOWN... "SECRETARIAL HELP WANTED: MUST BE BLOND, GREAT-LOOKING CHICK WITH DYNAMITE LEGS, AND..."

CLASSIFIED

HOLD IT, **HOLD IT!** YOU CAN'T SAY THAT! THE WOMEN'S LIB TYPES'LL BE ON US IN A FLASH!

YEAH, YOU'RE RIGHT.

MAKE THAT: "SECRETARIAL HELP WANTED: MUST BE BLOND, GREAT-LOOKING **PERSON** .... WITH DYNAMITE LEGS..."

CLASSIFIED

11

HAVE YOU HAD ANY EXPERIENCE WITH ANY OTHER COMPANY, LUCILLE?

OH YES.

THERE WAS THIS WEEKEND WITH B COMPANY AT FORT BRAGG...

THAT WAS AN EXPERIENCE!

LOOK... WHEN YOU ANSWER THE PHONE, LUCILLE... MAKE IT SOUND LIKE THIS IS A CLASSY OUTFIT—

— SOUND SOPHISTICATED... IT'S THE FIRST IMPRESSION THAT COUNTS.

RING

HELLO... WALL STREET JOURNAL...

HEY, LUCILLE! I GOTTA FLY TO CLEVELAND TOMORROW...

MAKE ME A RESERVATION, WILLYA?

RIGHT!

HELLO, CLEVELAND? DO YOU HAVE ROOM FOR ONE MORE?

MAGNELLY 5/1

PHEW!... I GOTTA WASH MY JOGGING OUTFIT BEFORE ROT SETS IN.

LAUNDROMAT

CLINK

THORP

FIRST TIME I'VE EVER SEEN A WASHING MACHINE THROW UP.

MAGNELLY 5/2

mā′·sŏn·īte

— a member of
a devout sect of
bricklayer.

SHOE, I HAVE FINALLY DISCOVERED THE PERFECT DIET BEER.

—TASTES JUST LIKE REGULAR BEER BUT 1/3 LESS FATTENING!

HOW DO THEY DO THAT?

THE CANS ARE 1/3 SMALLER

16

Once again we find it necessary to criticize <u>cats</u>.

TAP TAP TAP

This is a very difficult editorial for us to write.

TAPPA TAP

For many reasons.

TAP TAP

5/15 MACNELLY

WE'RE GETTING A BUNCH OF LETTERS ABOUT YOUR ANTI-CAT EDITORIALS, SHOE.

GREAT, LUCILLE.... SEPARATE THEM INTO LETTERS FOR AND AGAINST OUR POSITION, AND WE'LL PUBLISH A SPECIAL PRO AND CON PAGE.

MACNELLY 5/16

BETTER MAKE THAT A SPECIAL <u>CON</u> PAGE...

PRO   CON

UH-OH...

WELL, CADDY... WHICH IRON WOULD YOU SUGGEST?

MACNELLY 7/21

YOUR WEIGHT AND FORTUNE

5¢

KACHING!

GET OFF ME, YOU LOAD.

7/24 MACNELLY

MACNELLY 3/5

29

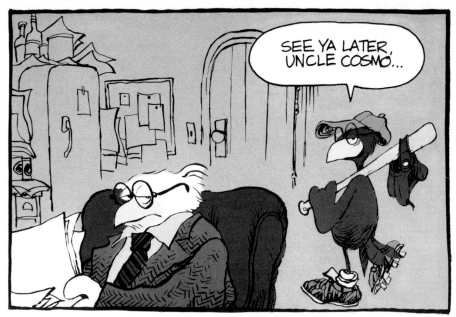
SEE YA LATER, UNCLE COSMO...

HOLD IT, SKYLER. WHERE ARE YOU GOING? HAVE YOU FINISHED ALL YOUR HOMEWORK?

YEAH... ALL BUT THAT PAPER WE HAVE TO WRITE.

WHAT'S IT ABOUT?

IT'S SUPPOSED TO BE A TEN-DAY DIARY OF A CIVIL WAR PRISONER...

34

43

49

I BETTER OPEN A NEW CAN OF BALLS FOR THE BIG MATCH.

OOPS... WRONG CAN.

WELL, THIS IS IT! MATCH POINT....

HERE GOES...

UMPH!

FOOM!

THIS LITTLE DOODAD IS GONNA HELP ME GET INTO THE U.S. NAVY...

I'VE RIGGED THIS CABLE AND HARNESS SO I CAN SWOOP DOWN THERE TO THE NAVY RECRUITING STATION...

WHEN THAT GUY SEES HOW GRACEFULLY I COME IN FOR A LANDING, HE'S BOUND TO LET ME IN THEIR PILOT TRAINING PROGRAM.

AND THEN THERE'S THE JUXTAPOSITION OF THE GEOMETRIC TO THE NATURAL —THE CLEAN PLANES OF MAN'S ARCHITECTURE CONTRASTING WITH THE UNDULATIONS OF NATURE'S CONTOURS.

BUT THEN THERE'S THE REAL REASON I'M PAINTING THIS BARN...

IT NEEDS IT.

MACNELLY 9/24

59

60

62

69

78

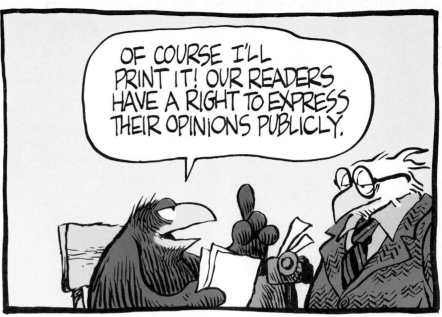

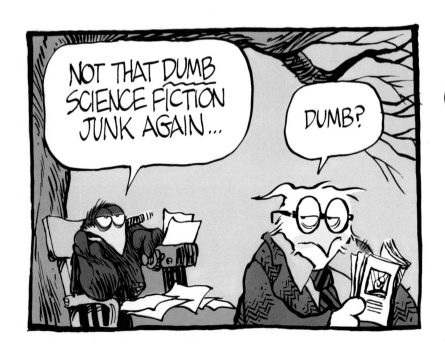

SCIENCE FICTION NOT ONLY ALLOWS US TO ESCAPE OUR ASSIGNED SPACE AND TIME...

AND STEP INTO OTHER DIMENSIONS.

IT LETS US EXAMINE OUR MUNDANE, EARTHBOUND PROBLEMS FROM A FRESH, ORIGINAL VIEWPOINT...

MACNELLY

THIS ISN'T COMIC BOOK STUFF HERE, SHOE! THIS IS **PHILOSOPHY**!!... MIND-EXPANDING, HEAVY PHILOSOPHY!!

"The Feast of the Khroobles"?

YEAH...

IT'S ABOUT THESE CREATURES MADE OF MEATLOAF WHO EAT TOLEDO.

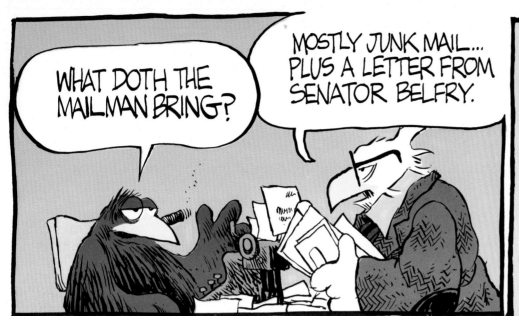

WHAT DOTH THE MAILMAN BRING?

MOSTLY JUNK MAIL... PLUS A LETTER FROM SENATOR BELFRY.

MAKE THAT ALL JUNK MAIL.

I WONDER WHAT SENATOR BELFRY WANTS FROM ME...

As a U.S. Senator, I believe it's important to maintain a dialogue with my constituents.

Therefore, I'd like to take this opportunity to share some thoughts with you on the pressing issues of the day.

Probably the most distressing development in recent years is the massive growth of our government.

As government grows larger and more and more impersonal, the average citizen finds himself more and more alienated....

He feels he is nothing more than a card in a vast computer – a number on some federal form.

Is there anything we can do?

Well, that's why I'm writing you today, Mr. Tribune....

WHAT'S THIS?

IT'S ALL WRINKLY...

OH, NO WONDER... IT'S A PRESS RELEASE FROM THE AMERICAN PRUNE COUNCIL.

HEY, SHOE... THE AMERICAN PRUNE COUNCIL IS HAVING A CONTEST

GOOD GRIEF! NOT A PRUNE-EATING CONTEST! BLECH!!

NAH, IT'S FOR "THE BEST EDITORIAL ON THE CONTRIBUTION OF THE NOBLE PRUNE TO THE AMERICAN WAY OF LIFE."

YOU WANNA ENTER?

It's time to get our currency back on a sound footing.

We must return to the old system and back the dollar with something of real, tangible value, like the gold standard...

3/5

or the glazed donut standard.

WHAT DO I LIE HERE?

WELL... LET'S SEE.

HMM...

CADDIES WITH POCKET CALCULATORS DON'T LAST VERY LONG IN THIS LEAGUE, PAL!

BIF

MACNELLY 8/5

LOOK, SHOE, WE CAN'T PRINT THIS LETTER— CHECK OUT THE LANGUAGE...

WELL, JUST EDIT OUT THE BAD WORDS AND WE'LL HAVE TO RUN WHATEVER'S LEFT.

Dear ~~darling Tom~~,
   I saw that ~~stupid piece~~ you wrote about ~~this nonsense~~ ~~affair~~ in ~~today's paper~~! You are a ~~useless~~ ~~snot~~!! And you can take your ~~stupid~~ newspaper and ~~shove it~~ ~~there~~!!
                              Sincer~~ely~~

MACNELLY 8/16

HOW ABOUT THAT! THE IRS IS GOING TO AUDIT ME...

GOOD GRIEF! THAT MEANS THEY'LL COME IN HERE AND SEARCH THROUGH ALL YOUR RECORDS!... AREN'T YOU WORRIED?

NAW!

I THINK BIG GOVERNMENT FINALLY BIT OFF MORE THAN IT CAN CHEW. (HEE HEE)

8/28

YOU DON'T SEEM VERY UPSET ABOUT THE IRS AUDITING YOUR TAX RETURN, PERFESSER...

NOPE...IT'S NOT BOTHERING ME.

I'M GONNA DO WHAT ANY AVERAGE CITIZEN WOULD DO WHEN UNCLE SAM CALLS...

— GRAB YOUR CHECK STUBS AND HEAD FOR CANADA.

8/29

95

GOOD GRIEF! IT'S SO DEPRESSING TO READ THIS STUFF.

DAY AFTER DAY, NOTHING BUT GREED, LUST FOR POWER, AND VIOLENCE.....WHY, IT'S GETTING SO BAD...

MACNELLY 9/12

I'M GONNA STOP READING THE SPORTS PAGE.

Memo:
To: P. Martin Shoemaker, Editor.
From: Cosmo Fishawk, Editee.
Subject: My desk.

TAP TAP

My desk is an intricate system of archives and reference material which has proven to be a valuable resource in our day-to-day journalistic tasks. Therefore, my desk and I would both appreciate it very much if you would...

MACNELLY 9/15

stop referring to us as "a compost heap of information."

98

Treetops, Va., Oct. 9, 1978.—

The campaign to unseat incumbent Senator Battson D. Belfry hit a new low today

with the opening of the headquarters of COTSITOBB:

The Committee to Sock it to Old Blubber Butt.

CORRECTION:

The advertisement on page two of yesterday's edition which read, "Color TVs $9.95," should have read, "Color TVs $499.95."

We apologize for any inconvenience caused by the riot.

IT SURE WOULD BE GREAT TO GET AUNT ROSE'S BENTLEY GOING AGAIN AFTER ALL THESE YEARS...

MAYBE I SHOULD TRY HER WAY OF GETTING IT STARTED. IT ALWAYS WORKED WITH HER...

HOME, BENTLEY.

Senate challenger Bilbo Barfnagel called a press conference for tomorrow afternoon at his headquarters.

The candidate has insured that this will be a major Media Event

by announcing free beer for all gentlemen of the press.

Senate candidate Bilbo "Biff" Barfnagel denied a report that his campaign is in financial trouble.

The denial was made at a surprise appearance at his headquarters

in Room 207 of the Downtown YMCA.

MACNELLY 10/26

HERE'S THE LATEST POLL, SENATOR, AND IT LOOKS BAD.

OH?

YEAH. THERE ARE 15% UNDECIDED, AND 85% DECIDED.

DECIDED WHAT?

THEY'VE DECIDED YOU'RE A FLAMING LIZARD.

MACNELLY 10/28

Reelect the ...ator

In a recent Tattler-Tribune poll of contributors to the "Biff" Barfnagel campaign, 42% of those polled thought they were giving to a worthy cause...

23% were members of the candidate's immediate family...

and 35% thought they were giving to a disease.

WILL YOU EVER GET MARRIED, UNCLE COSMO?

OH. I DOUBT IT, SKYLER. I ALMOST DID ONCE OR TWICE.

BUT NOW? WELL, I'M SORTA SET IN MY WAYS. IT WOULD BE HARD TO CHANGE.

WE LONG-TIME BACHELORS ARE MIGHTY FUSSY ABOUT THE WAY WE LIVE, Y'KNOW.

Classified Ads

PERSONALS

TO THE OWNER of the
Green Mercury wagon,
Lic. No. WA88K1:

your lights are on.

ROZ'S
ROOST
"JUST LIKE
EATING AT HOME."

ROZ'S
ROOST

EAT
YOUR
LIMA
BEANS

114

SHOE, DO YOU THINK THERE IS INTELLIGENT LIFE ON OTHER PLANETS?

HECK, NO...

WHY SHOULD OTHER PLANETS BE ANY DIFFERENT FROM THIS ONE?

Gasoline at Mr. Smith's station is 25¢ a gallon and at Mr. Jones' station it sells for 28¢ a gallon.

Jimmy pays $2.97 for 10.6 gallons. Where is Jimmy buying gasoline?

In 1958.

Dear Perfesser:
    My '63 Chevy makes an awful grinding sound, and it smokes and jerks a lot when I go over 20 mph.

MACNELLY 1/22

Is there anything on the market to get rid of my problem?

Yes. A tow truck.

Ask the Perfesser

Q: Is there any trick to raising chickens?

A: None at all. Just make sure that they get enough water,

MACNELLY 1/23

and plant them 8 to 9 inches apart.

YOU GOT ANY MORE TYPEWRITER PAPER OVER THERE? I'M ON MY LAST SHEET.

NOPE.

TURN IT OVER AND TYPE ON THE OTHER SIDE.

I DON'T KNOW WHAT GOOD THIS WILL DO, SMARTY.

Dear Editor:
    Am I nuts, or have your editorials deteriorated into nothing but name-calling insults?

You're nuts.

YUP...NO QUESTION ABOUT IT.

EITHER I NEED GLASSES...

MACNELLY 2/13

OR I GOTTA START SMOKIN' SHORTER CIGARS.

'Though you never send me flowers, and you hardly ever phone, I think of you most evenings When I sit here all alone.

My love for you, my darling, Makes my heart tick like a bomb. So until we meet again, dear...

MACNELLY 2/14

Wear your rubbers. Love, Your Mom.

120

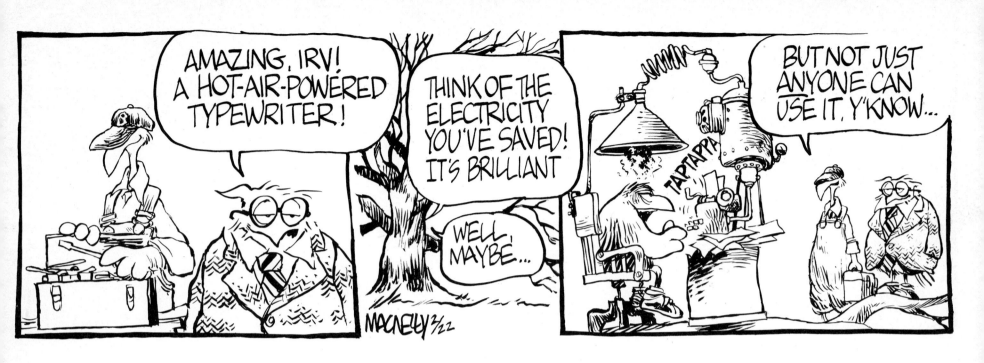